Dear Becky

Good luck with your new job. You will be amazing

Yours 'Bc.

GW01314742

INDUSTRIAL HISTORY OF THE LOWER RIVER LEA

A WALKING GUIDE
BY
ROB SMITH

Rob Smith
London

Copyright

Industrial History of the Lower River Lea – a Walking Guide

First published in 2020

The author and the publisher specifically disclaim any liability, loss or risk which is incurred as a consequence, directly or indirectly, of the use and application of any contents of this work.

ISBN 9798641636344

Copyright © 2020 Rob Smith

The right of Rob Smith, identified as the author of this work, has been asserted in accordance with The Copyright Designs and Patents Act 1988.

All rights reserved. No part of this work may be reproduced in any material form (including photocopying or storing by any electronic means and whether or not transiently or incidentally to some other use of this publication) without written permission of the copyright holder except in accordance with the provisions of the Copyright, Designs and Patents Act 1988.

Applications for the copyright holder's written permission to reproduce any part of this publication should be addressed to the publishers.

Copyright acknowledgements

All photographs used are the authors own

Other illustrations are all in the Public Domain

Every effort has been made to trace rights holders, but if any have been inadvertently overlooked, the publishers would be pleased to make the necessary arrangements at the first opportunity.

Contents

Introduction	8
1 Stratford Railway Works	10
The Early Days of the Railway in Stratford	11
Twentieth Century Expansion and Decline	11
2 Walter Hancock's Steam Bus	13
The Infant	13
Hancock's Later Vehicles	15
3 The Alexandra Temperance Hotel	16
4 Stratford High Street Station	17
5 The Great Eastern Railway Printing Works	18
6 Stratford Market	20
A Day In The Life of The Market	20
7 The Channelsea River	21
Silk Weaving	21
Calico Printing	22
Sewage Workers Cottages	24
8 Wiggen Mill	25
Fertiliser, Acid and Car Batteries	26
9 Abbey Mills Pumping Station	27
London's Sewage Problem	28
Bazalgette's Solution	28
The Pumping Station Today	29
10 Three Mills Lock	31
11 Bow China	33
12 Nicholsons Gin Distillery	34
13 The Tidal Mills	35
The House Mill	35
The Clock Mill	36
14 The Imperial Chemical Works	37
A Dream Of Clean Clothes	37

Advertising Pioneer	38
15 Congreve's Rocket Factory	39
Rocket Man	39
16 The Limehouse Cut	41
Creating a Canal From A River	41
The Great Entrepreneur	42
17 Stratford Gas Works	43
Gas Company Rivalry	44
Building the Gas Works	44
The Gas Works Memorial Garden	45
The Gas Works Offices	46
18 West Ham Power Station	47
18 Bidder Street	49
Bidder's Folly	49
A Lost Community	50
19 The Thames Ironworks	52
Mighty Shipbuilders	53
The Irons	54
The End of the Ironworks	55
Closing Thoughts	56
Further Information	57
Acknowledgements	58

INTRODUCTION

When people talk of Industrial History, London does not always spring to mind. In a recent English Heritage Map of Britain's Industrial Past, the only entry for London was in terms of the financial industry. The excellent museums at Ironbridge, Kelham Island in Sheffield, Beamish and in Manchester which celebrate Britain's Industrial past are well known. Sadly, industry in London has largely been overlooked. This to me seems an oversight – London was home to industry even before the Industrial Revolution.

The River Lea, as it flows through East London, had a particular concentration of industry. Some of this was because, up until the local government reorganisation of the 1960s, the Lea formed the outer boundary of London, a place where smelly and polluting industries that were not tolerated in central London, could be located. Despite the products that were made in the Lea Valley making fortunes for the traders in the City, few Londoner's would visit the Lea's industrial areas, unless they had business there.

Even today it is a difficult area to know well. South of Hackney, the Lea splits into numerous rivers and channels, many manmade to harness the power of the water. In this book, you will hear about two of the tributaries – the Channelsea River and the Three Mills Wall River, and a manmade canal, the Prescott Channel that connects them. Even the name of the River is confusing – it is known as both the Lea and the Lee, and part of the River is now a parallel canal called The River Lee Navigation. When I came to London in 1990, I found this area fascinating with its tangle of rivers and dark derelict buildings. Over the years the area has changed once more, with new housing built, and Stratford being at the centre of redevelopment in the wake of London 2012.

As I began to find out more about the area, I wanted to show other people the places that I had found so fascinating. In 2013 I developed a walking tour which connected many of the stories of the industries of the Lower River Lea and have been leading groups on the walk, one of the many tours I give with Footprints of London, the guiding group I helped form with my friends. I decided to make this book based on the walk for those who prefer to discover the area on their own, those that have walked with me but would like a recap, or those that simply prefer to follow the walk from their armchair.

This book is intended to help you find your way around the area between Stratford and Canning Town, passing through Bow and West Ham, highlighting the industries and businesses that were developed there. Some of the buildings, like the Abbey Mills Pumping Station, remain, some are long gone. I feel it is important that London's industrial history is celebrated even if it is just a memory.

You can enjoy this book without any need to do the walk itself, but I always feel that the best way to understand history is to walk it, to occupy the same space as people who have gone before. To follow the route read the instructions in italics. The walk is about three miles in total and can be completed in two and a half hours. The walk starts at Stratford Station and ends at Canning Town. There are opportunities to finish the walk at Bromley By Bow underground station or Star Lane Docklands Light Railway if you do not wish to walk it all in one go.

The walk is mainly easily accessible throughout the route. The path by the Channelsea River in section 10 can get a little muddy so boots would be advisable in wet weather or this section can be skipped by following the signs to Three Mills Island from the Greenway. The pavement in Bidder Street in section 18 can be very uneven with steep kerbs. You can avoid this by going direct to Canning Town Station following Stephenson Road.

1 STRATFORD RAILWAY WORKS

The walk starts at Stratford station where there are connections from all over London. To find the start of the walk follow the signs for Stratford Town centre from Stratford railway station. Leave the station by the exit nearest the Jubilee Line platforms. As you leave the station, in front of you is a red steam engine, bearing the name "Robert"

This walk starts by a railway engine, and the railway is important to Stratford's history. At its peak in the 1920's 6000 people worked making railway engines at Stratford. The steam engine called Robert that you see here today is something of an interloper, built in Bristol in 1933. Robert worked in an iron ore quarry in Northamptonshire for most of its working life, before spending time at the site of Beckton Gas Works a few miles east of here. Robert was moved to the current location after London 2012.

THE EARLY DAYS OF THE RAILWAY IN STRATFORD

The railway came to Stratford in 1839 when the Eastern Counties Railway built a line from Stratford to Mile End, which was then extended to Bishopsgate. Early railway engines required a lot of maintenance work, and so in 1840, a large roundhouse, similar in design to the famous Camden Roundhouse, was built at Stratford. This allowed trains to be repaired under cover, and the revolving turntable in the roundhouse meant the trains could be moved onto other tracks once they were repaired. Tragically the Stratford Roundhouse, designed by Robert Stephenson was demolished as recently as the 1980's.

Expansion came in 1847 when railway mogul George Hudson bought 15 acres of land to build and maintain railway engines for his expanding empire. In addition to the railway works, homes were built for the workers, rows of houses that became known as Hudson Town. Those that worked in the Stratford Railway works were highly skilled – in 1891 they constructed a complete steam engine in 9 hours 41 minutes! These skilled workers were well organised, in 1861 they set up their own Co-Operative movement which allowed them to buy food in bulk which they sold affordably in their Co-Operative shop, one of the first such shops in the South of England.

TWENTIETH CENTURY EXPANSION AND DECLINE

In the 1920s the Stratford site expanded to 24 acres, and by the 1950s it had grown to 78 acres with 6000 workers. Many of the workforce were women, who specialised in making things like the upholstery for the seats in the carriages and blinds for the windows. By the 1980s the workers in Stratford had built 1682 locomotives, 5500 carriages for passengers and 33,000 goods wagons.

Despite all the experience of railway engine building, with the end of steam locomotives, British Rail wanted to concentrate on other centres of train building like Derby and Crewe, and train production in Stratford ended in 1963. Tragically the magnificent industrial buildings were cleared from the site in the 1970s. The site is now occupied by Westfield Shopping Centre. To get an idea of what could have happened to Stratford Railway Works, take a trip to Swindon where the old works has been converted into a shopping centre and railway museum, which would have been more interesting than the current Westfield buildings.

2 WALTER HANCOCK'S STEAM BUS

Walk past Robert and keep the Jubilee line platforms to your right. On the left is Stratford bus station, with its long sculpture of green and yellow fish like shapes. Keep walking until you get to a footbridge, but do not cross over it.

You are looking at one of the largest bus stations in East London, decorated by London's longest sculpture – "The Stratford Shoal" designed by Studio Egret West in 2011. The shimmering green and yellow shapes are meant to remind us of a shoal of fish. The bus station is sited on another place connected with steam powered transport that was here even before the railways.

THE INFANT

In 1824 Walter Hancock built an experimental steam powered vehicle at a site near Stratford High Street. The first vehicles were small, while Hancock worked on a boiler that was less likely to explode, but by 1829 he had developed a ten seat bus known as "The Infant", which was used for a regular service between Stratford and London. The machine was powered by coke and had a crew of three – driver, stoker, and brakeman.

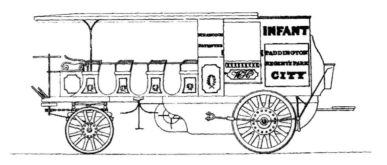

In 1831 Hancock wanted to further demonstrate the capabilities of the Infant by taking it on a journey to Brighton. With much excitement the passengers on board left Stratford bound for London at the breakneck speed of 16 mph, and all was going well by the time they crossed Blackfriars Bridge, bound for the little village of Streatham. However, as they climbed up the North Downs the speed began to drop to a mere 5 mph. The quality of coke in the countryside was not as good as that in the city, causing the power of the engine to drop. When the adventurers reached Hazeldean in the Sussex Weald they decided to stay at an inn for the night, while messenger boys were sent out looking for supplies of coke.

With fresh supplies on board The Infant set out for Brighton the next day. Its arrival on the seafront seems to have created quite a stir but there was no time to linger, after two trips along the esplanade the journey home began. Unfortunately, one of the wheels broke on the return over the South Downs and this proved terminal, the passengers had to return to London by horse drawn coach. The test had proved successful though – one writer said, "We reached Brighton in not too much discomfort, and no one was scalded". The repaired Infant returned to London but ran into difficulty when the citizens of Streatham barricaded the road to prevent it travelling through the village. This was a sign of the hostility to steam powered vehicles that would come later.

HANCOCK'S LATER VEHICLES

After the success of The Infant, Hancock (left) built bigger vehicles at Stratford. In 1833 the fourteen seat Enterprise began service between Paddington and the City via Islington, and then in 1836 the 22 seat Automaton was introduced, capable of a respectable 20 mph. A test journey made it as far as Birmingham. However, in a story that will become familiar on this walk, Hancock had built up enemies among the owners of horse drawn coaches, who then petitioned Parliament to put ever steeper tolls on steam powered vehicles, which, by 1840 made Hancock's business unviable. Hancock continued as inventor, but the technological advantage he had built up with road vehicles had been lost.

3 THE ALEXANDRA TEMPERANCE HOTEL

Continue along Station Street towards a building with yellow window frames and then left along a little path called Farthingale Walk which will take you out onto Stratford High Street next to a modern sculpture.

The sculpture is called "Railway Tree" made by Malcom Roberts in 1996, a tree shape made of curved railway tracks that remind us of Stratford's railway past.

Across the road is the Discovery Story Centre, which started life as the Alexandra Temperance Hotel, designed by S. B. Russell in 1901. Temperance hotels were built across London as places where workers could find accommodation free from the temptations of alcohol. This hotel had room for 200 people, in 42 bedrooms with first- and second-class dining rooms, a palm court with its own string quartet and a billiard room. It is possible that train drivers who had been sent to pick up new steam engines might have been accommodated here to ensure they stayed sober for the journey. In World War One it was home to the officer's mess for the West Ham Battalion, and many soldiers would have spent their last night in England there before being sent to the front line. Today the Discovery centre is a great place to combine reading books and play, ideal if you have younger children to amuse.

4 STRATFORD HIGH STREET STATION

Cross the road and walk right, past the Discovery Centre and continue along the road until you reach Stratford High Street station.

The station was originally opened as Stratford Bridge station in 1847, then rebuilt as Stratford Market station in 1892 and then closed in 1957. It was reopened as part of the Docklands Light Railway in 2011.

Before the station opened the area was home to makeshift yards making things that were to smelly and polluting to be made in central London. Being East of the River Lea meant that Stratford was outside the jurisdiction of the new London County Council who had created restrictions on things like glue making going on in their area.

One of the businesses was a builder's yard called Rivett's where a huge fire started in 1855. The alert was brought by an apprentice who had seen a glue pot catch fire in the building he was working in, but the boy became trapped by flames. A plasterer attempted to rescue him put was trapped when a beam from the roof fell on him. Soon the whole yard was ablaze. The local Stratford fire engine was called but this was not sufficient to put out the fire and Stratford residents had to form a chain of buckets to try to extinguish the blaze, nearly a thousand people in total helped. Eventually the fire is put out and the boy and the plasterer saved when two engines from the London Fire Brigade arrive. Sadly, with every industrial innovation, come new industrial accidents, which are all too common without proper laws to protect health and safety.

5 THE GREAT EASTERN RAILWAY PRINTING WORKS

Continue a short way along Stratford High Street and then left into Burford Road. On your left is a tall brick warehouse building.

This fantastic old industrial building was originally part of the Great Eastern Railway Printing Works, built in 1893 and one of a pair, the other having been demolished.

Why did the railway own a printing works? To print posters, timetables, and railway tickets. If you look at the top of the building you can see the well-lit spaces that artists worked in. They designed posters for locations on the railways network, like Lowestoft, and made them look attractive destinations for tourism.

Timetables were obviously especially important to the early railways. With different train companies operating on shared routes, having a timetable to coordinate trains was vital. Timetables were printed here for every station on the Great Eastern Network, and the first British Rail timetable was printed here in 1948.

Railway tickets were also essential when, as now, railways were run by different companies. A journey from one side of the country to another might involve travelling on a number of trains from different companies, but the fair was paid at the first station. To ensure each company got paid for their part of the journey, passengers would have their ticket clipped on each train they travelled on, and at the end of the journey their ticket was collected and inspected for the individual companies clip marks, so that the fair could then be divided up among the different railway companies. Printed tickets were therefore key to the railway's profits, hence owning a printing works. It is nice to see one of the companies currently occupying the building is a printer.

6 STRATFORD MARKET

Continue along Burford Road. At the end of the road is the entrance to Stratford Market Depot, to the right of the gate is a path where you can see through the fence into the depot.

In front of you is Stratford Market Depot, where Jubilee Line trains spend the night being serviced, repaired, and cleaned. It was designed by Wilkinson Eyre and completed in 1996, and is described as a "super shed", 100m wide and 190m long.

The depot is built on the site of Stratford Market which was opened in 1886. The market was one of the responses to London's rapidly rising population during the nineteenth century. Between 1850 and 1900 London's population doubled from three to six million. You could not continue feeding a population that size by bringing food from the country on horses and carts. London needed food on an industrial scale, bringing food by the trainload to wholesale markets like Stratford Market. In total the market handled 100,000 tons of vegetables a year, which were then distributed out to shops and retail markets.

A DAY IN THE LIFE OF THE MARKET

The first train of the day was the Whitemoor Vegetable Express, which arrived at 4.15 am. This carried the most time sensitive items like peas and broccoli from Cambridgeshire. Later in the day would come more durable foods like potatoes from Lincolnshire. Goods would also arrive from London's docks, Stratford Market was used by Fyffes as the main distribution centre for bananas. In the 1950s a weekly service using a train ferry via Zeebrugge was planned to bring food from Europe.

As motor transport improved, rail distribution centres like Stratford Market became less popular and by the 1980's the sidings closed, and were used for a number of years for storing old railway trains, until the Jubilee line extension proposed reusing the site.

7 THE CHANNELSEA RIVER

Retrace your steps back along Burford Road and then turn left into Cam Road, keep following this around to the right until you see a path on your left called Channelsea Path which is next to a block of flats called Burford Wharf apartments. Turn left onto this path until you get to some little sculptures of ladybirds and other insects.

At this point the River Lea is split into three tributaries, and you are standing on top of one of them - the River Channelsea. It is an underground river at this point, but you will see it above ground later in the walk. The river here was buried in the 1960s but if you look on the right-hand side of the path you can see part of the old riverbank, where barges would have been moored. Though this is a humble location today it has a very important part in London's Industrial History

SILK WEAVING

The first mention of silk weaving by the Channelsea goes back to 1594, probably using raw silk from Italy, and the trade seems to have flourished in the 17th century, largely due to the import of silk from India. What is interesting though is that in 1675 a Frenchman is said to have had an engine loom here – a machine that could weave several ribbons at once. A machine, possibly powered by water, based in a dedicated building outside someone's home. This sounds very like a factory – built nearly a century before Richard Arkwright's mill in Cromford, Derbyshire, which is often cited as one of the first factories of the Industrial Revolution.

Stratford's technological lead was not to last long though. The machine loom caused concern for the silk weavers of Spitalfields, and in 1675 a mob of 2000 weavers descended upon Stratford and begin smashing the machine looms. The militia had to be brought in to quell the riot and the ringleaders were put on trial. I their defence on of them said

> "one man with an engine loome can do more work in one day than ten men with ordinary loomes – we are so desperate we would rather hang than starve".

The riots seem to have succeeded in stopping the silk weaving trade as there is no mention of it by the Channelsea after 1675.

CALICO PRINTING

No sooner than weaving Indian silk had ended though, another material from India became the mainstay of a different textile industry, calico printing. Calico was a coarse, cheap cotton material, printed with colourful designs in Calcutta and imported to Britain to make more affordable clothing, than could be made from silk. This proved a threat to the homegrown wool industry and so in 1700 an act of parliament banned the import of printed calico. However, unfinished grey calico was still allowed to be imported and a man called William Sherwin took out a patent on a method to print designs on calico at his factory near the Channelsea. The clothes were hung out to dry in an area which is still marked as the Calico Grounds on 19th century maps.

Once again, the Spitalfields weavers were unhappy about this. In 1719 they began a campaign of throwing ink over any woman who was seen wearing printed calico dresses. The calico printers also received threats for employing labour from outside London – in 1750 Richard Newman is given a death threat for employing Irish workers when Englishmen were starving for lack of work.

Textile work in London went into a decline in the latter half of the 18th century. New machinery to spin cotton grown on slave plantations in America made Indian cotton less competitive. The steam powered machinery used needed coal that was more readily available in the North of England, along with water supplies and a damper climate that aided spinning cotton. By 1830 only one calico printer remained by the Channelsea, a company called Burford and Sons, which went on to make dyes, hence Burford Road that you walked along earlier.

Look carefully by the side of the path and you will see some of the mooring rings used to tie up barges when this area was used by calico printers.

SEWAGE WORKERS COTTAGES

Continue walking along the Channelsea Path, and in about five minutes on the right-hand side you will see a charming row of houses.

The cottages in Abbey Lane are an exceptionally fine example of accommodation built for workers, but then the workers here had a ghastly job – working on part of London's sewage system, the Abbey Mills Pumping Station, which you'll see shortly. They were built in 1865.

With industry on its banks and crowded housing nearby the Channelsea was a highly polluted river with an outbreak of cholera occurring in 1857.

8 WIGGEN MILL

Return to the Channelsea Path and continue until you cross Abbey Lane. On the other side of the road you will see the Channelsea River emerge to the surface. Continue up the steps or ramp until you get to a path called The Greenway which crosses the Channelsea River on a bridge. Go left on to the bridge and look across the river on the far side of the bridge where you will see an island in the river.

The little island in the Channelsea is another early industrial site. The Domesday Book of 1086 records seven mills in this area, and the one on the island was called Wiggen Mill – which is probably taken from the name of the Saxon owner Wicga. The mill became the property of Stratford Langthorne Abbey (hence the area being known as Abbey Mills). The mills in this area were used by the bakers of Stratford to grind wheat into flour, and they used wood from Epping Forest to fire their oven to bake bread that was sold in London. Stratford loaves proved very popular – so much so that, in 1307 the Assize of Bread and Ale set rules saying a Stratford loaf had to be larger than a London loaf but could only sell for the same price. This put up the costs to Stratford bakers but was not a deterrent to buyers, so eventually Stratford bakers were only allowed to sell one cart load of bread in London per day, which restricted the amount Stratford Bakers could sell. The mill on the island lasted until as recently as World War Two when it was destroyed by a bomb.

FERTILISER, ACID AND CAR BATTERIES

To the left of the island, the site that is currently vacant was home to Thomas Bell and Company. They were manufacturers of "artificial manure" – phosphate fertilisers - on the site from 1870-1882. The process of making phosphate fertiliser had been perfected by John Bennet Lawes in 1837 and involved treating animal bones from London's butchers with sulphuric acid. As part of the process Thomas Bell and Co had part of the factory here for producing sulphuric acid, or oil of vitriol as it was known. Thomas Bell and Co were bought out in 1882 by a company called F W Berk and the site focused on making sulphuric acid, for use in electricity generation and later car batteries. During the 1950s nearly all the car batteries in the UK were produced at this site, known as Pacific Wharf.

It was a fearfully dangerous process. One worker at Berk's said he saw a leak appear in one of the sulphuric acid storage tanks but knew the leak would be contained by a protective wall around the tank. To his horror the wall dissolved before his eyes, and tons of sulphuric acid poured into the river. The leak killed all the fish in the river for miles around. During World War Two the War Ministry took over the island, leading to rumours among the workers that they were developing a deadly acid-based weapon. F W Berk continued as Berk Spencer Acids until the 1980s.

9 ABBEY MILLS PUMPING STATION

Trace your steps back over the bridge along the path known as The Greenway to take a look at the Abbey Mills Pumping Station on your left. If you walk a little way along, the fence is lower allowing a better place to get a view and take photographs.

You are looking at a building known as the "Cathedral of Sewage", built 1865-68 to designs of architect Charles Driver, as part of the sewer system created by Joseph Bazalgette. Cathedral is just one way of describing it – the building is built on a cross shape like a Byzantine church, the slate roof could be from a French Chateau , some of the windows look like they are from an Italian Medieval church and it once had two minaret like chimneys. The purpose of the building was to raise sewage from one of the lower level sewer pipes, up to the higher level sewer you are standing on.

LONDON'S SEWAGE PROBLEM

There had been a sewer system in place in London during the Tudor period, with sewage pipes emptying into the Thames. When London's population was small this system coped but with a population of 3 million in 1850, dumping sewage into London's river became dangerous. With some of London's drinking water being drawn from the Thames, and other water supplies being polluted by cess pits, it was not surprising there were outbreaks of water borne diseases like Typhoid and Cholera. In 1832 a cholera outbreak killed 30,000 people in London and further outbreaks in 1854 killed another 10,000.

Unfortunately, the link between dirty drinking water and disease had not been clearly made in the 1850s. It was believed that ill health was caused by a miasma, an invisible foul cloud that floated above London, created by decaying organic matter from cess pits, graveyards, and butchers waste. The foul stench rising from the polluted Thames was taken as proof of the miasma theory, and campaigners like the scientist Michael Faraday called for the Thames to be cleaned up.

BAZALGETTE'S SOLUTION

The final straw came in August 1858, in what became known as the Great Stink. The smell from the Thames was so bad, Parliament was unable to sit, despite dipping the curtains in chlorine to keep back the smell. Metropolitan Board of Works engineer Joseph Bazalgette was commissioned to develop a scheme to clean up the Thames and end the stink.

Bazalgette's scheme, a revival of an earlier scheme designed by Frank Foster, involved building intercepting sewers that ran West to East, collecting the waste from the Tudor era sewers. The waste was washed along by water from London's underground rivers like the River Fleet, flowing by the power of gravity to two outfall stations at Beckton on the North of the river and Crossness on the South side. You are standing on the Northern Outfall Sewer. Two other lower level intercepting sewers converge at Abbey Mills and the pumping engine was built to raise the sewage in these up to the level of the Northern Outfall Sewer. This was initially using steam powered pumps, which was why the site had the two minaret style chimneys. You can still see the bases of the chimneys either side of the main building.

From Abbey Mills the sewage washed along the Northern Outfall Sewer to Beckton, where it was held in a large tank until the tide was on the way out. Then it was dumped into the Thames and the tide carried London's human waste on its way out to the sea. This cleaned up the Thames in London but was not so good for places further down the river like Gravesend and Southend. Bazalgette was never happy with this part of the solution, and shortly after his death, the system changed. Sewage was loaded onto a boat at Beckton and taken out to the North Sea and dumped there. Nonetheless Bazalgette's sewer system is a remarkable achievement – after it was built there were no more Cholera outbreaks in London, and it still serves us well.

THE PUMPING STATION TODAY

The building ran on steam power until the 1930s when electric pumps replaced them. This rendered the tall chimneys redundant and they were demolished during World War Two. It was feared that if they were hit by a bomb they might collapse and land on the pumping station. Londoners could take a lot during the Blitz, but the toilets failing might have been the final straw!

In 1997 a new pumping station was built – a silver building which you can see behind the current building, and Driver's 1868 building became a backup pumping station. It is still an important part of London's infrastructure, so not generally open to the public, but worth looking out for on Open House London events in September. The wrought iron interior is quite spectacular. It has also been used as a film set, playing the part of Arkham Asylum in the 2005 film "Batman Begins".

Retrace your steps towards the bridge, to where there is a gate in the fence on the right, near where you can see a metal spiral painted to look like a snail.

The "snail" is part of one of the original pumps used to raise sewage to from the lower level sewers to the higher level pipe. If you listen carefully you can hear rushing water – sewage from the City of London being pumped by modern equipment to join sewage from Clerkenwell.

10 THREE MILLS LOCK

Continue past the "snail" pump and follow the path down the ramp with the yellow rail. You will find a path that goes beside the Channelsea River. Keep walking along this path for about five minutes. On the other side of the river, on the left-hand side you will see the brown painted round gas holders, you will get a closer look at them later in the walk. Eventually the path bends round to the right and you will see a large lock. Walk along the path until there is a bridge over the lock, then turn left and pause on the bridge.

You are now standing over another part of the River Lea - this time a manmade part of it called the Prescott Channel. It is named after Sir William Prescott, who was head of the Metropolitan Water Board when the channel was dug in the 1930s. The idea of the channel was to control flooding in the area. In the 1960s the channel was widened and lined with rubble, some of which came from the demolished arch which once stood outside Euston Station.

The Three Mills Lock is the largest working lock in London and it was built as part of the construction of the 2012 Olympics site – the idea being it could carry construction barges to the site in Stratford. Unfortunately, there were delays in constructing the lock, partly caused by finding a 2000kg unexploded bomb from World War Two at the bottom of the channel, and the lock has rarely been used. It serves another purpose though – if there had been a sewage leak during the Olympics, the lock gates would have prevented polluted water getting to the Olympic Park.

11 BOW CHINA

Cross the bridge and follow the path around the left side of the green space in front of you. Walk towards another river where a large number of canal boats are moored up.

This is another tributary of the River Lea - the Three Mills Wall River. On your right you will see Bow Bridge – carrying Stratford High Road over the river. It was here, in the 18th century that one of London's most important ceramic industries was based – the Bow China Works.

Bow China started with an idea by Thomas Frye, a talented artist from Dublin, who had gained prominence after painting a portrait of the Prince of Wales. He was unimpressed by the reliance on imported porcelain that the East India Company was importing from China, adversely effecting Britain's balance of payments. However, the Chinese were not keen on parting with the secret of porcelain manufacture, so Frye had to reverse engineer the production of porcelain. In 1744 he took out a patent on material which

"allows china exceeding goodness and beauty than that which is imported from abroad".

The secret ingredient was a material called China Clay. The only problem was that the only source of China Clay at that time, was in the lands of the Cherokee Native Americans, so Frye's first porcelain was expensive to produce.

Production took place at a factory on this site known as New Canton, 300 workers produced everyday things like plates, dishes, and mugs. Frye also made porcelain figurines, often of popular actors and actresses from the theatre, that acted as a showcase for the quality of his company's products. Some of these are on display in the British Museum.

In 1768 China Clay was discovered and extracted in Cornwall which changed the dynamics of ceramic making. In 1776 the Bow China works moved to Derbyshire, and the centre of the porcelain making industry moved up to places like Stoke on Trent, but it started here in London.

12 NICHOLSONS GIN DISTILLERY

Continue left along the Three Mills Wall River until you get to a sculpture of two clasping hands.

The sculpture, called "Helping Hands" made by Alec Peever, commemorates workers who collapsed and died at Nicholson's Gin Distillery in 1901. J&W Nicholson moved to this site from Clerkenwell in 1873, making their famous Lamplighter Gin. In 1901 Thomas Pickett was asked to go down a well in the distillery to measure its depth. As soon as he reached the bottom of the well, he collapsed. The factory manager, Godfrey Nicholson, was sent for and he descended the well and he too collapsed. Two more men Fred Elliot and Robert Underhill also went down the well and collapsed before it was decided to call the fire brigade. Luckily, the London Fire Brigade had a new piece of equipment – the fume hood, which allowed them to go safely into down the well. Sadly though, all four men were found dead. It was thought that noxious gasses had built up in the well, possibly from contaminated land – another reminder of why health and safety laws are so important.

13 THE TIDAL MILLS

Walk a short distance to the left and you will see another river join the Three Mills Wall river, and to the left you will see the rear of the tide mill. Keep a look out for herons which often walk the muddy bank at low tide.

The tide mills at Three Mills are remarkable, the largest tide mills in Europe and a proud survivor of the many mills on the River Lea. The tide mill worked by making use of the big difference between high and low water on this part of the river. If it is low tide look for the green line on the river wall showing you where high tide is. When the tide is high sluice gates in the mill shut and the water stored in the area you are looking at now, added to by water from the Three Mills River and the other channel of the River Lea you see joining in front of you. When the time was right the sluice gate was opened and the pent-up water rushed through, powering the mill wheel.

THE HOUSE MILL

Walk along the river and turn round the corner to your right. You are standing between the two tide mills, the House Mill on your right and The Clock Mill on your left.

There have been tide mills on this site since medieval times, when they were used to grind flour for bread making. The current mills foundations date back to 1380. In the 1580s they were used for the making of gunpowder, for the war against Spain. In the 18th century they began to be used in the manufacture of gin. The mill on your right, The House Mill was rebuilt in 1776 by Daniel Bisson, look up on the wall and you can see his initials DB on his family cartouche. The building was used for gin production up until World War Two. By the 1970s the building was in a terrible state and was due to be demolished. It was saved by the Passmore Edwards Museum Trust and is now a Grade 1 listed building. A trust now looks after the building and has a long-term plan to restore the mill to working order. The Mill is open for tours most weekends in Spring and Summer and has an excellent café.

THE CLOCK MILL

The current Clock Mill was built in 1817, again for gin distilling, for an MP, Philip Metcalfe who owned the distillery. The beautiful oast house roofs give the building an appearance which is surprisingly rural for East London. The cowl at the top is designed to turn the roof to catch the wind, allowing smoke to escape from a grain drying kiln below. When the tide was right the mill could grind as much as 14 tons of barley on one tide, with the equivalent power to an 150hp engine. The largest of the mill wheels was 8ft wide. Of course, high tide can come at any time of day, and so the millers had to be ready to work through the night. To supplement the two tide mills, there was also a windmill – hence the area being known as Three Mills Island. Today the Clock Mill is used as a Science School and the rest of the site is a film studio - site of the original Big Brother House.

14 THE IMPERIAL CHEMICAL WORKS

If the café at House Mill is open, you may wish to take a break here. Alternatively, there are toilets and a coffee machine at the Tesco supermarket across the bridge. Bromley by Bow London Underground Station is also a short distance from here if you wish to complete the walk another time.

The Tesco on the other side of the river is on the site of the Imperial Chemical Works – a factory founded by the soap powder manufacturer Harper Twelvetrees

A DREAM OF CLEAN CLOTHES

Harper Twelvetrees was born in Biggleswade in 1823, and at the age of 16 was appointed manager of his family's stationery firm. However, his first love was chemistry, and Twelvetrees got up at 3.30am each day to study chemistry textbooks, before going to work in the shop at 6am. At the age of 25 he had a dream – to produce a soap powder that could be sold cheaply enough everyone to afford to buy it. After all, having dirty clothes was a bar to self-advancement – if you worked in places like Smithfield Market or the London Docks, and could not clean your clothes, you would be excluded from getting work in other places. Many places of accommodation stipulated that you needed clean clothes to be a resident. And, of course dirty clothing was unhygienic.

Twelvetrees first soap factory was in Islington, but in 1858 he moved it to this site in Bow, moving his family into a house formerly owned by the tide mill manager. Selling small penny packets of soap was a success, and the factory went on to make, polish, starch, baking powder, Epsom salts – even clothes washing and wringing machines.

HARPER TWELVETREES' WASHING MACHINE.

Twelvetrees believed in good conditions for workers – he ordered cottages for his workers families to be built on site. There was a library and a lecture programme for workers, a sickness benefit scheme, and a pension fund. Social activities included sewing meetings, a brass band, and a cricket club.

ADVERTISING PIONEER

While Harper was useful to Londoners by getting their clothes clean, another of his innovations they might not thank him for. Twelvetrees believed in advertising his soap powders, using painted signs on buildings, brightly coloured catalogues and notices in newspapers. All of this was highly novel at the time – Twelvetrees competitors were dismissive of his needing to "boast" about the benefits of his products.

Sadly, while his business did well in Britain, an expansion into the United States was not so successful, his business partner swindling him out of a fortune, and Twelvetrees was forced to sell the site at Bow. Nonetheless he paved the way for affordable ways of cleaning clothes.

15 CONGREVE'S ROCKET FACTORY

Continue along the path between the two rivers, with the tidal River Lea on your left, and the non-tidal River Lea Navigation on your right. In about five minutes you will pass underneath a railway bridge that carries the District Line and trains to Fenchurch Street over the river. Pass under the bridge and look across the River Lea to the brown gas holder frames on the other side of the river.

Before the gas holders across the river were built, the site was occupied by William Congreve's Rocket Factory. In 1780 the forces of Indian ruler Tipu Sultan used rockets against East India Company troops at the Battle of Pollilur, to devastating effect. After the eventual defeat of Tipu Sultan, the British captured some of his rockets, and the rocket scientists that built them and sent them to the Royal Woolwich Arsenal for investigation. There Sir William Congreve (below) was given the task of evaluating the military potential of rocket technology.

ROCKET MAN

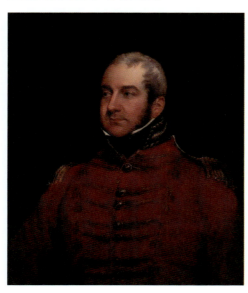

After an initial lack of interest Congreve persuaded the Royal Navy that rockets would be ideal for use from ships. In 1805 an attack was launched on the French port of Bolougne with Congreve's rockets launched from boats. A few of the rockets hit the target, but many of them were blown off target by the wind – right into the course of a French frigate! A lucky hit maybe but it meant that the rockets were used again in the war against America in

1812. The American Fort McHendry came under bombardment by Congreve's rockets (below) – an event recorded in the American national anthem, where the lines -

> "And the rockets red glare and bombs bursting in air
>
> Gave proof through the night that our flag was still there"

refer to rockets that may have been built on this site. Rockets were also used at the Battle of Waterloo, where mostly they simply scared horses. Congreve also made fireworks that marked the peace after the battle had ended. Long term however, the British Military chose not to develop rocket technology after 1862 and the factory closed, to be replaced by the gas works. Who knows what might have happened if Britain had carried on building rockets?

16 THE LIMEHOUSE CUT

Continue on the path with the tidal River Lea on your left and the canal boats of the River Lea Navigation on your right. When you get to a road bridge follow the ramp with yellow handrails up to the midway level, where there is a block to sit on.

From here you get a good view of Bow Lock where the tidal River Lee begins a wild series of loops on its way to the Thames. Over to the right you can see the Limehouse Cut, which is a canal linking with the Thames and the Regent's Canal.

CREATING A CANAL FROM A RIVER

As you will have noticed the River Lea has a big drop between high and low tides. That combined with the twists and turns the river makes between this point and the Thames made it hard for boats to navigate. During the 18th century the River Lea was increasingly being used for transporting grain, as well as gunpowder from the Royal Gunpowder Mills in Waltham Abbey, and it became obvious that improvements would be needed to make the river more navigable.

The first stage was for the engineer John Smeaton to carry out a survey in 1765. He proposed creating a canal to run parallel with the River Lea – the River Lee Navigation, and at the Southern end, to bypass the bends of the river by digging a new canal – the Limehouse Cut. This would link up with the Thames at a wharf owned by timber trader Charles Dingley. Dingley had a great interest in getting the canal open, it would enable him to ship timber up the Lee Navigation to the burgeoning furniture making industry in Hackney, as well as being a route into Hertfordshire and Essex where wealthy men were building country houses that needed timber.

Dingley started work on the Limehouse Cut in 1770 but the work was plagued with problems like bridges and canal walls collapsing, and by 1777 it was found to be too narrow for the amount of traffic travelling on the canal, so the Limehouse Cut was doubled in width.

THE GREAT ENTREPRENEUR

Charles Dingley had an amazing career, trading with the chaotic court of the Tsar of Russia during the 1730's and opening up overland trade routes between St Petersburg and Persia. He owned sugar refineries in Russia and had a monopoly on importing brushwood into London. His timber yards made him wealthy, but what made him wealthier still was investing in the New Road – a toll road that connected Westminster to the City – London's first Ring Road, that we now know as Marylebone Road, Euston Road and City Road. He also dabbled in politics.

Perhaps most interestingly though Dingley worked on a way to saw wood into planks by using wind power. The wind powered sawmill was completed and started to be used at his Limehouse wood yard. It was not long before the sawyers of London saw this as a threat to their livelihood. A picture of Dingley sawing through Magna Carta was produced to illustrate how dangerous this new technology was. In May 1767, a mob pulled the sawmill to the ground. Once again, the innovation in the Lea Valley was stifled by vested interests.

17 STRATFORD GAS WORKS

You will leave the River Lea now. Continue up the ramp and turn right to cross the River Lea on the road bridge. On the other side of the bridge a path leads down to the riverbank. This walk does not go that way, but if you wish to take a detour to look at the arts centre at Cody Dock you can take that path. Instead go straight on to look at the brown gas holders on the left-hand side of the road.

Gas holders like the ones in front of you were once a common site in cities across Britain, but they are increasingly under threat as gas is no longer stored in the huge tanks that the gas holders were built to support. Some have been repurposed, most famously those at King's Cross which have been incorporated into new flats. The gas holders at Stratford Gas works are even nicer – look how the decorative designs of the ironwork are all different.

GAS COMPANY RIVALRY

Gas power really took off in London as a result of the work of Frederick Winsor, who demonstrated gas powered street lighting in 1807. By the 1830s, demand for gas had increased – gas lit factories could work twenty-four hours a day, while homes lit by gas meant that activities like reading and sewing were possible on long winter nights. A new competitor for Winsor's company appeared in 1837 – the Commercial Gas and Light Company - soon numerous local gas companies were battling for control of territory. The worst incident occurred in 1850 where the Great Central company and the Commercial companies' workers ended up fighting each other on Bow Bridge, after each had tried to sabotage their rival's pipelines.

BUILDING THE GAS WORKS

Stratford Gas Works was started in 1846 by the West Ham Gas Company, and at that time was one of the largest in London. The gas storage cylinders are only a small part of a gas works. Gas works relied upon a large supply of coal and that was brought in by barge to the site that is now the Cody Dock Arts Centre. From there it was brought by a narrow-gauge railway to the retort. The retort was a tall building which burnt coal in a furnace and the resultant biproducts like tar and ammonia were filtered off for sale to the chemical industry. The coal gas produced from the burnt coal was sent to the storage cylinders. Another biproduct of the process was coke which could be used as a fuel, but it required storage before sale, taking up more of the site. The process also produced poisonous residues that needed removal, requiring more space. Not surprisingly this meant that gas works were huge sites, and you will be walking through the site of the Stratford gas works for the next ten minutes.

Developing the Stratford Gas Works cost the West Ham Gas Company a large amount of money, and it would be a long time before shareholders would recoup their investment. This led to the company being taken over by their rivals the Gas Light and Coke Company in 1910. The Gas Light and Coke Company owned the even larger gasworks at Beckton, which gave them economies of scale that cut production costs

THE GAS WORKS MEMORIAL GARDEN

Continue along Crows Road for a few metres with the gas holders to your left. On the right-hand side of the road there is a wooden fence with a gate in it. Go through the gate in the fence and down a path with some steps in it and you will be in a garden with some memorials and a statue in it.

This unexpected little garden houses memorials to the workers of the Gas Light and Coke Company in both World Wars. The column features an eternal gas flame – a fitting memorial. There is also a statue of Sir Corbett Woodall – the governor of the Gas Light and Coke Company. Woodall was involved not only in gas but the provision of hydraulic power across London, an entrepreneurial engineer. However, it is a bit of an indignity for the West Ham Gas Company to have a statue of the head of the rival Gas Light and Coke Company built on their own land after the hostile takeover in 1910!

THE GAS WORKS OFFICES

Walk past Corbett Woodall's statue across the grass to the road and turn left. Just to the left you will see a building marked London Gas Museum

This was the administration centre for the Stratford Gas Works, and for a while The London Gas Museum, though sadly it closed down some time ago, the collection moving to Leicester. Outside you can see the emblem of the Gas Light and Coke Company – this was originally on the wall of the Beckton Gas Works before the building was demolished – during the filming of Stanley Kubrick's film Full Metal Jacket, where it stood in for the streets of Saigon.

18 WEST HAM POWER STATION

Continue along Twelvetrees Crescent to the roundabout and then go on past the Menzies distribution centre until you get to some metal gates. Go through these. Twelvetrees Crescent becomes Cody Road here. Continue along Cody Road for about five minutes until you get to a café on the left-hand side. On the right-hand side you will see a large electricity substation owned by UK Power Networks.

All the land you have walked on since the Gas Works Office was part of the Stratford Gas Works – demonstrating the size of the site. Its neighbour was the West Ham Power Station, the electricity substation in front of you is all that remains of this power station.

West Ham was a large borough in Essex until 1965, with its own council. The borough council decided to get in on electricity generation and opened a series of small power stations which proved inadequate for demand, so in 1904 a new power station was opened on this site. West Ham borough had sizeable network of electric trams which were power hungry, and electric street lighting also contributed to the demand. By the 1920's they had another customer – the nearby Royal Docks, which needed power for refrigerators, cranes and lighting. This led to an expansion of the power station – all before the more famous Battersea

Power Station had opened. Heavy damage occurred in World War Two, but the power station was extended in the 1950s. A large coal fired power station in a built up area became increasingly undesirable however, and so by 1983 the site was completely closed after a long decline (in which it was used as a location for the Michael Caine film "The Ipcress Files").

18 BIDDER STREET

Continue along Cody Rd until you get to the junction with Stephenson Street. You will see Star Lane DLR station in front of you. Turn right into Stephenson Street and walk along until you get to the junction with Bidder Street South

These two roads are named after railway engineers who worked together on some of Britain's early railway network – Robert Stephenson and George Parker Bidder. Bidder Street is one of the oldest streets in the area known as Canning Town, an area that grew up to provide accommodation for the families of dockworkers and those that worked at the Thames Ironworks

BIDDER'S FOLLY

In 1847 George Parker Bidder started work on a new railway from Kent to London, which took a rather unusual route. Passengers travelled through Kent as far as Woolwich, where they disembarked to take a ferry across the river to North Woolwich where they joined another train that took them on a route through the West Ham Marshes to Stratford. People wondered why Bidder had built a railway through an uninhabited area, and the line became known as Bidder's Folly. The route is still used today by the Docklands Light Railway trains that travel through Star Lane.

Not long after the railway was completed, there was a need for a new dock for London – one large enough to accommodate the new steam ships that were arriving in the port. There were only a limited number of places that a dock of this size could be built – the most obvious one being the West Ham Marshes. Who owned the land around there? George Parker Bidder and his railway. The investors that built the dock, which became the Royal Victoria Dock, had to take Bidder on as a partner and Chief engineer in order to get hold of the land. The railway did not look such a folly after all.

A LOST COMMUNITY

Turn right into Bidder Street South and continue until you are near the entrance to the scrap metal yard on the left.

Bidder Street today is almost totally devoted to recycling industries, dealing with scrap metal and building waste. Although Bidder Street is far from attractive, all cities need the type of businesses that operate here. It was not always like this though, until World War Two Bidder Street was a busy community with people living in rows of terraced houses on either side of the street which were built in the 1850s.

The houses were very poorly built, in an area of marshy land they were subject to subsidence and damp, and pictures of them in the 1890s show them being propped up by scaffolding. There were no proper sewers – ironic in view of their proximity to Bazalgette's sewer pumping station, and ill health and poverty were rife. Charles Dickens describes the area in "Household Words" in 1857 -

> "Canning Town is the child of the Victoria Docks. The condition of this place and of its neighbour prevents the steadier class of mechanics from residing in it. They go from their work to Stratford or to Plaistow. Many select such a dwelling-place because they are already debased below the point of enmity to filth; poorer labourers live there, because they cannot afford to go further, and there become debased."

The reports from school inspectors to the local board school describe children bare foot dressed in rags, showing signs of starvation.

We know some of the names of people who lived in Bidder Street from the Census and Street Directories. Where you are standing is where Nicholas Charlton, an Iron moulder originally from Newcastle, and his wife Rosetta and their 8 children lived at 76 Bidder Street in 1891. Just down the street, Fred Goodwin had his butchers' shop and Harry Scotton ran the fried fish shop. It is sad to think that all sign of this community has vanished without trace. It all came to an end in one devastating night in 1940 when the whole street was flattened in an air raid. The houses on Bidder Street were never rebuilt, and it became the industrial street that you see today. Maybe one day Bidder Street will be rebuilt with riverside apartment blocks, and all trace of the scrap metal businesses will be gone too.

19 THE THAMES IRONWORKS

Continue along Bidder Street, if it is a weekday, watch out for lorries turning into the scrap metal yards. At the end of the street turn right into Wharfside Road and follow the underpass beneath the busy road. At the end of the underpass turn right and walk to an area of seats with a view of the River Lea.

You are back on the banks of the River Lea now, at the point where the river takes a long meandering series of loops to get to the Thames. The Lea flows underneath the blue bridge to your left for half a mile, then doubles back on itself to the other side of the DLR tracks, then passes under the red bridge, before doubling back, then making a final loop into the Thames. So, this is a good spot to have a bridge, the most recent one being the Lower Lea Crossing you have just passed underneath.

A more elegant bridge existed before. In 1810 a new iron bridge over the River Lea was built by the engineer James Walker, similar in design to the famous bridge built by Thomas Telford 30 tears earlier at the place we now know as Ironbridge. This bridge was unfortunately hit by a barge in 1887. It was replaced by another bridge, which was made using steel made at the Thames Ironworks. You can see the brick abutments of this bridge to the left of you.

MIGHTY SHIPBUILDERS

The area around the mouth of the River Lea had been a centre for shipbuilding for hundreds of years – the Blackwall shipyards building fast sailing ships for the East India Company. In 1837 the Thames Ironworks opened (originally under the name Ditchburn and Mare) to build a new generation of metal skinned ships. Initially building paddle steamers, the Ironworks went on to build the Royal Navy's first metal skinned ship, HMS Warrior in 1860. The 4000 workers went on to build ships for the Danish, Spanish, Ottoman and Romanian navies, as well as ferries, tugboats, freighters and lifeboats. By the 1890's the yard had grown to occupy both banks of the river at the site you are standing at.

BIRD'S-EYE VIEW OF THE THAMES IRONWORKS SHIPBUILDING YARD, SHOWING TWO WARSHIPS UNDER CONSTRUCTION.

THE IRONS

In 1890 Arnold Hills became manager of the Thames Ironworks. The trade unions were becoming stronger in the London Docks, and Hills was determined to keep unions out of the Thames Ironworks. He believed that if workers were given a good working environment, they would not need trade unions. One of the innovations Hills introduced was an 8-hour working day, which was a short shift at the time. He also encouraged a worker's football team, Thames Ironworks FC, who played in the Southern League and the FA Cup. By 1900 the money involved in football was rapidly rising – one club paid £50 to sign a new striker! The team's players pushed for Thames Ironworks FC to turn professional to be more competitive. Arnold Hills was reluctant to do this, as he saw the club as a ship workers club. The players decided to form their own breakaway club, which became known as West Ham United. If you look on the West Ham badge today, you will see two crossed ship workers hammers, with the letters TIW on them – short for Thames Iron Works. The outline of the badge is a cross section of HMS Warrior. West Ham fans still call the club The Irons.

THE END OF THE IRONWORKS

This spot must have been an awe inspiring place to be standing in the 1890s – the sight of huge ships under construction, the deafening noise of rivets being hammered and steel plate being rolled, the smoke and smell of the work going on. A new ship being launched always attracted a big crowd. In 1895 this had tragic consequences at the launch of HMS Albion. 30,000 people arrived to watch the Navy's new ship being launched, but despite being told not to get too close to the ship, many crowded around to get a look. When the ship rolled down the slipway a wave washed some spectators into the water – leading to 34 people drowning.

The last ship to be completed in the Thames Ironworks was another warship – HMS Thunderer, built in 1910 as part of the arms race between Britain and Germany. This vast super dreadnaught warship tied up the whole of the Thames Ironworks for nearly a year, meaning other ships could not be built during that time. HMS Thunderer did not generate much profit for the Ironworks – the ship was meant to be built out of sense of patriotic duty. Larger shipyards on the Clyde and the Mersey were better suited to building large warships, and no more orders from the Royal Navy followed. The Ironworks diversified into producing cars and aero engines, but it was not enough to save them, and the Thames Ironworks closed down in 1912. You can still see HMS Warrior today, a floating Museum in Portsmouth Harbour, part of the Historic Dockyard there – but built in London, by Londoners and something that Londoners should be proud of. While a trip to Portsmouth is a great day out – you can also see a part of HMS Warrior much closer to hand.

Retrace your steps back to where the underpass under the Lower Lea Crossing wa,s but instead of going back through the crossing carry on straight on up some steps to a pavement by the side of the busy Lower Lea Crossing and turn right towards Canning Town Station. Cross over the entrance to the bus garage by the pedestrian crossing then turn right and go into the station. Just through the door you will see a large metal plate.

The metal plate is part of the hull of HMS Warrior, moved here as a memorial when the Jubilee Line extension was built in 1999.

CLOSING THOUGHTS

I hope you have enjoyed this walk through East London's industrial past. So many fantastic pieces of innovation have come from this little piece of London, textiles, ceramics, iron working, railways and ship building among them. It is a shame that there is not a better memorial to the industrial endeavour of the workers in these factories, but I hope this walk, at least in part, acts as one.

FURTHER INFORMATION

Books

Belton, Adrian. The Thames Ironworks – a History of East London Industrial and Sporting Heritage. 2015 The History Press

Dobrasczyk, Paul. Into The Belly of the Beast – Exploring Victorian London's Sewers. 2009 Spire Books

Harrison Daniel. The Thames Ironworks – A Major Shipbuilder on the Thames. 2015 Crossrail Archaeology

Korr, Charles. West Ham United -The Making of A Football Club. 1986 Gerald Duckworth

Lewis, Jim. Industry and Innovation – the technological revolution in the Lea Valley. 2010 Libri Publishing

Marshall, Geoff. London's Industrial Heritage. 2013 The History Press

Newham Parents Centre. A Marsh and a Gasworks: One Hundred Years of Life in West Ham. 1986 Newham History Workshop

Pedroche, Ben. London's Lost Power Stations and Gas Works. 2013 The History Press

Pewsey, Stephen. Stratford a Pictorial History. 1993 Philimore

Powell, WR. A History of the County of Essex Vol 6. 1973 Victoria County History

Film

Kelly, Paul. What Have You Done Today Mervyn Day? 2005

Websites

Newham Photos https://www.newhamphotos.com/

Footprints of London https://footprintsoflondon.com

Cody Dock https://codydock.org.uk/

ACKNOWLEDGEMENTS

Many thanks to Steve Hanshaw, Rebecca Howard, Russell Challinor, Mark Tindley and Ben Franks for plodding London streets with me over the years, which was the initial inspiration for becoming a guide. Thanks to Simon Bradley for providing lots of London information. Lots of people encouraged me to write a book, but particular thanks to Colette Mason for practical help setting things up, also Sue Davies, Marion Watkinson, Matt Brown, Janet Smith, Tina Baxter, Marie-Eve Menger, Alex Ionescu, Hazel Baker, Roberta Arden, Kathy Smith, Peter Henning, Amber Raney Kincade, Laura Agustin, Adenike Johnson, Jenni Bowley for good ideas and inspiration. Many thanks too to the many people who come on my walks – I appreciate the support of every one of you, but Catherine Dauvergne, Andrew Mahoney, Jen Pedler, Sheila Cavanagh, Candice Pettifer, Kathryn Prevezer and Anne Tickell have always come up with kind words when it counted. Thanks too to my sons Tom and Albert Davies-Smith who have often been involved in route testing, occasionally against their will.

Printed in Great Britain
by Amazon